DRAW FUTURE WORLDS

By Bryan Baugh

LOWELL HOUSE JUVENILE

LOS ANGELES

NTC/Contemporary Publishing Group

Published by Lowell House
A division of NTC/Contemporary Publishing Group, Inc.
4255 West Touhy Avenue, Lincolnwood (Chicago), Illinois 60646-1975 U.S.A.

Managing Director and Publisher: Jack Artenstein
Director of Publishing Services: Rena Copperman
Editorial Director, Juvenile: Brenda Pope-Ostrow
Director of Juvenile Development: Amy Downing
Typesetter: Treesha R. Vaux

Lowell House books can be purchased at special discounts when ordered in bulk for
premiums and special sales. Please contact Customer Service at:
NTC/Contemporary Publishing Group
4255 W. Touhy Avenue
Lincolnwood, IL 60646-1975
1-800-323-4900

Printed and bound in the United States of America

Library of Congress Catalog Card Number: 98-66657

ISBN: 1-56565-925-2

10 9 8 7 6 5 4 3 2 1

CONTENTS

This book shows you how to draw 22 futuristic characters and objects. Before you begin, here are some tips that every aspiring artist should know!

- Each illustration includes step-by-step instructions to help you as you draw. Keep in mind that the final step features only one way the drawing can be finished. Use your imagination to make each alien, monster, and vehicle your own creation! Note: The bolder lines in each drawing step point out the parts of the drawing that are being added.

- Use a large sheet of paper and make your drawing fill up the space. That way, it's easy to see what you are doing, and it will give you plenty of room to add details.

- When you are blocking in large shapes, draw by moving your whole arm, not just your fingers or your wrist.

- Experiment with different kinds of lines: Do a light line, then gradually bear down for a wider, darker one. You'll find that just by changing the thickness of a line, your whole picture will look different! Also, try groups of lines, drawing all the lines straight, crisscrossed, curved, or jagged.

- Remember that every artist has his or her own style. That's why the pictures you draw won't look exactly like the ones in the book. Instead, they'll reflect your own creative touch.

- Most of all, have fun!

WHAT YOU'LL NEED

PAPER

Many kinds of paper can be used for drawing, but some are better than others. For pencil drawing, avoid newsprint or rough paper because they don't erase well. Instead, use a large pad of bond paper (or a similar type). The paper doesn't have to be thick, but it should be uncoated, smooth, and cold pressed. You can find bond paper at an art store. If you are using ink, a dull-finished, coated paper works well.

PENCILS, CHARCOAL, AND PENS

A regular school pencil is fine for the drawings in this book, but try to use one with a soft lead. Pencils with a soft lead are labeled #2; #3 pencils have a hard lead. If you want a thicker lead, ask an art store clerk or your art teacher for an artist's drafting pencil.

Charcoal works well when you want a very black line, so if you're just starting to draw with charcoal, use a charcoal pencil of medium to hard grade. With it, you will be able to rub in shadows, then erase certain areas to make highlights. Work with large pieces of paper, as charcoal is difficult to control in small drawings. And remember that charcoal smudges easily!

If you want a smooth, thin ink line, try a rolling-point or a fiber-point pen. Art stores and bigger stationery stores have them in a variety of line widths and fun, bright colors.

If you are drawing on colored paper, you may want to experiment with a white pastel pencil. It creates bright highlights when combined with a black pen or a charcoal pencil.

ERASERS

An eraser is one of your most important tools! Besides removing unwanted lines and cleaning up smudges, erasers can be used to make highlights and textures. Get a soft plastic type (the white ones are good), or for very small areas, a gray kneaded eraser can be helpful. Try not to take off ink with an eraser because it will ruin the drawing paper. If you must take an ink line out of your picture, use liquid whiteout.

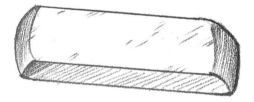

OTHER HANDY TOOLS

Facial tissues are helpful for creating soft shadows—just go over your pencil marks with a tissue, gently rubbing the area you want smoothed out.

A square of metal window screen is another tool that can be used to make shadows. Hold it just above your paper and rub a soft pencil lead across it. Then rub the shavings from the pencil into the paper to make a smooth shadowed area in your picture. If you like, you can sharpen the edge of the shadow with your eraser.

You will also need a pencil sharpener, but if you don't have one, rub a small piece of sandpaper against the side of your pencil to keep the point sharp.

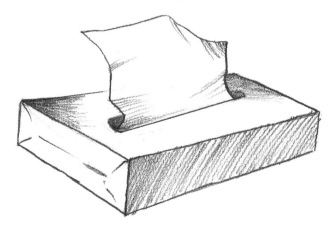

As you'll see with the characters and objects in this book, artists can use different drawing techniques to make their pictures unique. Here are some useful techniques for giving your drawings style and personality.

HATCHING

Hatching is a group of short, straight lines used to create a texture or a shadow. When you curve the hatching lines, you create a rounded look. This is handy when texturing a creature's curved body parts or underside. When you draw the hatching lines close together, you create a dark shadow. For very light shading, draw the lines shorter, thinner, and farther apart.

CROSS-HATCHING

This technique gives your character an even more shaded look. Start with an area of hatching, then crisscross it with a new set of lines. Compare the picture at right to the hatching drawing above to see how cross-hatching creates darker shadows and texture.

STIPPLE

When you want to give your drawing a different feel, try the stipple technique—all you need are dots! This method works best with a pen, because unlike a pencil, a pen will make an even black dot just by touching the paper.

The stipple technique is very similar to the way photos are printed in newspapers and books. If you look through a magnifying glass at a picture in a newspaper, you will see very tiny dots. The smaller and farther apart the dots are, the lighter the area is. The larger and closer the dots are, the darker the area. In your drawings, you can make a shadow almost black just by placing your stipple dots close together.

SMOOTH TONE

By using the side of your pencil, you can create a smooth texture on your drawing, shown here. Starting with the areas you want to be light, stroke the paper very lightly and evenly. Put a little bit more pressure on your pencil as you move to the areas you want to be darker. If you want an area even smoother, go back and rub the pencil marks with a facial tissue, but rub gently! If you get smudges in areas you want to stay white, simply remove them with an eraser.

Now that you're armed with the basic drawing tools and techniques, you're ready to get started on the drawings in this book.

Throughout this book, you can use the techniques that are shown with each of the drawings or you can make up your own—it's up to you!

TIPS ON COLOR

Your picture will stand out from the rest of the crowd if you use these helpful tips on how to add color to your masterpiece!

TRY WHITE ON BLACK

For a different look, try working on black construction paper or art paper. Then, instead of pencil, use white chalk, white pastel pencil, or poster paint. With this technique, you'll need to concentrate on drawing the light areas in your picture rather than the dark ones.

TRY BLACK AND WHITE ON GRAY (OR TAN)

You don't need special gray or tan paper from the art store for this technique. Instead, try cutting apart the inside of a grocery bag or a cereal box. This time, your background is a middle tone (neither light nor dark). Sketch your drawing in black, then use white to make highlights. Add black for the shadows.

TRY COLOR

Instead of using every color in your marker set or your colored pencil set, try drawing in black for shadows, white for highlights, and one color for a middle tone. This third color blended with the white creates a fourth color. You will be surprised how professional your drawing will look.

These gigantic Astro Cruisers patrol the galaxy, carrying squadrons of Fighter Blaster ships and legions of Space S.W.A.T. Soldiers wherever they are needed.

1 First, draw this big spaceship's basic shape.

2 Draw two circles on the front of the cruiser. Add a series of horizontal (some of them curved) lines throughout the body of the ship. Shape the front cockpit.

3 Add tail fins to the rear of the ship. Continue to detail the front of the ship. Erase unnecessary lines.

4 Draw curved vertical lines going down the side of the cruiser to suggest paneling. Also, give the cruiser bent, fork-shaped exhaust pipes that stick out along the lower rear side. Draw a row of tiny attached squares along the front of the cockpit for windows. Add four circles across the nose of the ship for portholes. Finally, draw a curved horizontal line along the bottom of the cruiser to suggest an undercarriage.

5 Add a few more details, then finish the cruiser with cross-hatching and shading. To make it feel even more real, add random dents and scratches all over the hull of the ship. This spaceship has traveled many light-years on many missions. Asteroids have bounced off it. Shooting stars have streaked by and left burn marks on it. Draw rusted areas on the ship to show that it has a history. Many small, scattered marks from your pencil are all it takes to imply this.

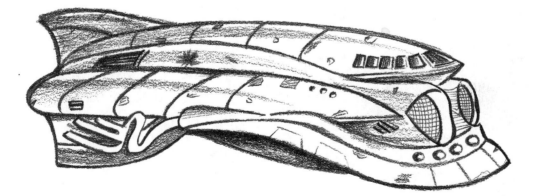

Vicious Lobster Monsters hide in caves and wait for their hapless prey to come along. Then they jump out and grab their victim. Worst of all is the Lobster Monster's nasty eating habit: It picks apart live prey with its pincers and eats the poor creature one little piece at a time.

1 Start the basic shapes of its head, torso, and abdomen with three circles. Add a guideline cutting through the two left circles to give you the curve of its spine.

2 Use simple lines inside the far-right circle to create the shape of its open mouth. Add guidelines for its arms and legs, marking all joints with circles. Begin the basic shapes of its pincer claws and feet with curved lines.

3 Draw sharp teeth in its mouth. Go around the whole shape of its body with zigzag lines to imply the monster's thick fur. Begin to shape its arms and legs with a solid outline. Create its sharp pincer claws with zigzag lines as shown. Make as many sharp edges as you wish—just be sure they're big and ugly!

4 Erase unnecessary lines. Detail the Martian Lobster Monster's arms and legs, then add long, crooked antennae. Draw a pair of eyestalks sprouting right up from the top of its head. Put little circles on the ends of these stalks for its eyes. Go around its jawline with another jagged line. Finally, add its curly tail.

5 Add details to the monster's eyes, eyestalks, antennae, and tail as shown.

6 To finish the creature, fill in its mouth and shade the antennae. You can detail as much as you wish. Bumps, knots, and ridges around its legs, arms, and pincers will suggest a rough, bumpy crustacean-shell texture.

Without a doubt, the Gross Grub Zero Beast is the most disgusting creature in the galaxy. One look at the beast will make the average person throw up on the spot, giving this dreadful monster the perfect opportunity to gobble up its poor grossed-out victim!

1 Draw an oval for the beast's head. Add a guideline to mark the center of its face. Next, draw the upside-down pear shape of the body as shown.

2 Create two small ovals for the eyes. Connect them to the head with short lines. Draw guidelines for the four tentacles that grow around its mouth.

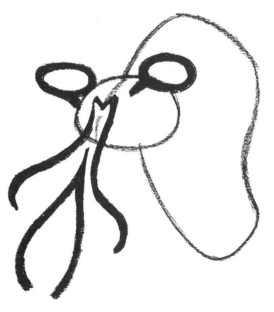

3 Build up the top of the head with another curved line above the first oval. Draw the outlines of its four tentacles. Use guidelines to start its legs, marking the joints with circles. Sketch in simple shapes for the feet.

4 Put pupils in its eyes, and create the outlines of its eyestalks, cheeks, and mouth. Next, fill its mouth with sharp little teeth. Separate its back and chest with a question-mark-shaped line that runs from its jaw to its hip. Outline the forms of the legs and feet. Erase the guidelines in the head and lower tentacles.

5 Draw the eyelids. Create arms, joints, and claws with guidelines and circles. Put in one curved line for its shoulder and one that goes down the center of its chest and belly.

6 Outline the forms of the arms and claws. With guidelines, draw the antennae with circles at the joints. The beast's back is a plated, segmented exoskeleton-type shell. Sketch in angled lines going down the back, one after another. Use zigzag lines along the insides of the mouth tentacles for even more teeth. Erase the lines in the legs and any extra lines in the top tentacles. Add further details to legs, feet, and eyes.

7 Erase the extra lines in the arms. Now it's time to detail your gross creature! Add spines, spikes, teeth, and any other details you wish. Use smooth shading around its body and appendages, especially down its back. Darken the inside of its mouth, eyes, and nostrils. Be sure to add segmented rib lines across its belly.

Bizarre but harmless, this flying creature populates the skies of several planets. A Flapdactyl's favorite food is garbage, which makes these foragers quite welcome in the large cities of space.

1 Start with an oval for the Flapdactyl's head. Draw a slightly curved line for its spine.

2 Draw a line across its face. Put a circle on either end of this line for its eyes. Using the spine as a guide, draw a body shape. From each of its shoulders, draw the long, arched lines of its wing bones.

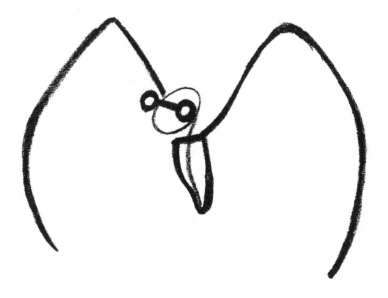

3 Shape its long snout and mouth as shown. Begin the small birdlike legs with tiny *V*-shaped lines on its body. Draw the first of its three tails. Sketch three lines branching out of each wing as shown.

4 Erase the line between its eyes, add its pupils, and form the outline of its bulging eyes. Draw the inner line of its lower jaw. Add three talons to each of its legs to create its feet. Give the Flapdactyl another curving tail. Use zigzag lines to create the webbing of its wings. Don't forget to complete the three small *V*-shaped wing talons.

5 Erase unnecessary lines. Detail the wrinkles of its eyelids. Further render its head, feet, and legs. Use zigzag lines around its neck and body to make it look furry. Give it one more tail, then erase unneeded lines in each tail. Sketch two more lines inside its wings to show the shape of the bones inside.

6 Fill its wings with crooked branching lines—blood vessels. Draw a series of short curved lines going around its legs, feet, and three tails.

7 Shade the Flapdactyl all over, making the inside of its mouth the darkest area. If you want to give your creature really wild skin, now is the time to do so using shading and hatching.

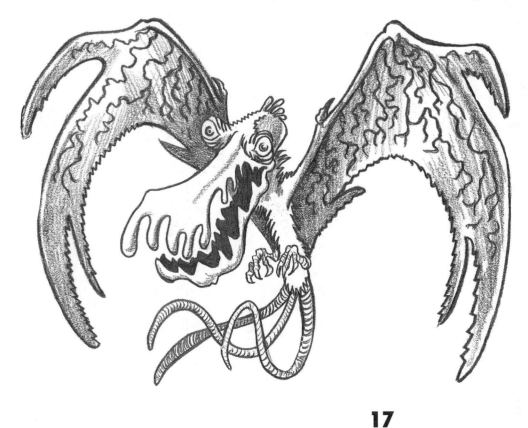

SPACE S.W.A.T. SOLDIER

These guys get paid to patrol strange new planets and deal with problems caused by dangerous alien creatures.

1 Draw the oval shape of the soldier's head. Place guidelines inside the oval. Create simple shapes for his upper body and hips. Draw a line from his neck to the base of his spine.

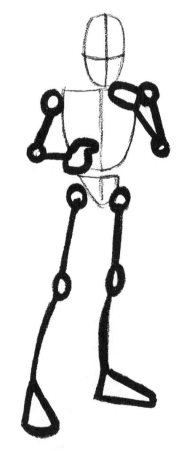

2 With guidelines, create his arms and legs. Use small circles for the joints and simple shapes for the hands and feet.

3 Sketch his eyes, nose, and mouth. Begin to form his helmet. Outline the guidelines with simple shapes to form his arms, legs, and shoulder pads. Connect his upper and lower legs with small rectangles. Shape his left foot.

4 Erase unneeded lines in his legs, face, and lower torso. Begin to detail his head with goggles, cheekbones, and a shaped chin. Place a radio antenna on his helmet, and use simple lines to define the shapes of his uniform. Start to define both feet. Add the soldiers's holster, on his right side, as well as his bag, which rests on his left thigh.

5 Erase the remaining unneeded lines. Continue to detail the soldier's head covering, gloves, boots, holster, and knee pads. Use a ruler to make a straight line for his rifle, which he is holding in both hands. Also add the strap for his bag.

6 Complete his rifle with simple shapes for the barrel and strap. Refine his goggles and uniform as shown.

7 Add shading as you wish, darkening some areas more than others. Use both hard and soft hatching to define the many details of the soldier.

A six-wheeled buggy for bouncing your way across the super-rough, rocky terrain of most moons, this little vehicle has the best, bounciest shocks in the universe!

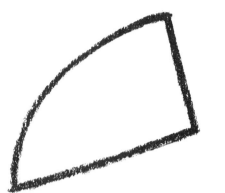

1 Start by drawing the shape for the side of the vehicle. It's almost a triangle, except one side is curved.

2 Draw the same shape again, only smaller, inside the first shape. This will be the side window. Next, add a curved rectangle for the front of the vehicle.

3 Draw the headlights, then attach them to the vehicle. Begin to create the grille on the front using tiny boxes.

4 Use rounded squares for the big all-terrain tires, as well as the area below each headlight. Attach them to the car. Put long *S*-shaped lines across the windows to suggest light reflecting off the glass.

5 Draw three more tires, and add detail to the two front tires. Define the undercarriage of the vehicle with pipes and shocks.

6 Put a number on the side—whatever number you want. Continue detailing the undercarriage, wheels, and tires, and use slanted lines for the tire treads. Draw jagged, rocky ground under the vehicle.

7 Add slanted lines for the tire treads on the last three tires. To finish, shade using hatching. Place lots of lines on the ground to create rocks. Detail the headlights with cross-hatching. Little lines, dots, marks, and shapes all over the body of the car will make it look dented and dirty. After all, this is a car built for rocky, dusty terrain. Make it look like it has seen some action!

This superfast Zip Car is the fastest in the galaxy and can outrace the Fighter Blasters any day.

1 Start with a long and slightly curved triangle.

2 Add one small triangle to the top and another slightly larger triangle to the side of your original shape. These form the tail fin and wing of the Zip Car.

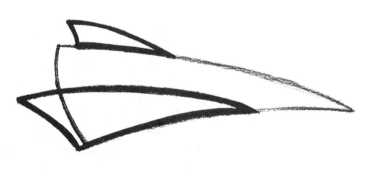

3 Erase unneeded lines in the body of the car. For the cockpit windows, add a pair of thin, curved triangles. Put a big speedy-looking *Z* along its side. Add a line down the middle of the wing and a pair of thin semicircles to the back of the wing for small engines. Then sketch in two half-circles on the wing side.

4 Draw a big thruster engine on the back of the car. Write the words *ZIP CAR* along the wing, and add small antialien guns to the front edge of the wing. Outline the *Z* along the car's side.

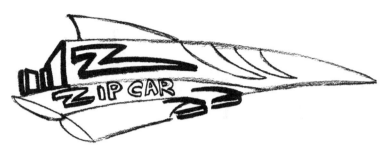

5 Detail your Zip Car with light shading and hatching. Make some areas dark. Don't forget to draw fire coming out of the rear engine. Add any finishing touches you wish.

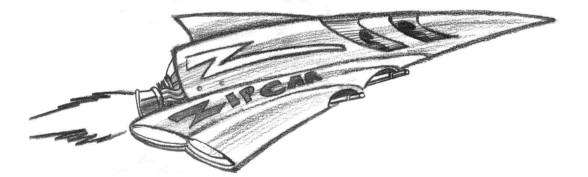

Dino Dogs are favorite pets all over the galaxy. As their name implies, they are half dinosaur, half dog. Smart, playful, and friendly, Dino Dogs have no natural enemies. Everybody loves Dino Dogs.

1 Start by drawing the basic shape of its head and the curving line of its spine.

2 Next, draw a double line for its mouth and a guideline to show the center of its face. Sketch circles for its eyes. Also, draw large circles for its visible shoulder and hip, connecting them to form its body.

3 Add a nostril, teeth, and lines for its neck. Sketch guidelines for its legs and small circles for its joints. Draw rounded shapes for its feet.

4 Erase the unneeded hip and shoulder lines. Add pupils in its eyes, curved guidelines for its big floppy ears, and a series of curving lines to make its wagging tail. Further detail its face, and create wiggly lines down its left cheekbone. Give the dog top teeth and a tongue. Fill out the shapes of its legs, and sketch ovals for its toes. Draw a collar around its neck.

5 Erase the lines inside its legs and body. Use simple curved lines to finish its ears. Darken inside its mouth. Add details, including scales, plates along its back, a tiny bone-shaped license tag on its collar, and nails on its toes. Don't forget the motion lines for the dog's tail.

6 Continue to detail the Dino Dog with bumpy scales and whatever else you wish using hatching and cross-hatching. You can give your creature a name by putting it in the bone tag. Don't forget to detail its eyeball, and leave the outer area of its eye black.

DR. OCTAGON HEX

The most evil man in outer space, Dr. Octagon Hex is a mad scientist determined to take over the galaxy and become its supreme ruler. He has started many battles, but so far has been beaten by Lord Squid Von Squood's Space S.W.A.T. Soldiers every time. For now, Dr. Hex hides in his secret laboratory, where he continues to make his wicked plans.

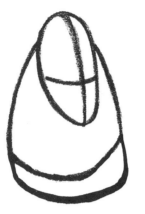

1 Create an oval for the basic shape of his head. Draw guidelines on his face to help place his facial features later. Add a basic pear shape for his upper body with a wide band along the bottom of it.

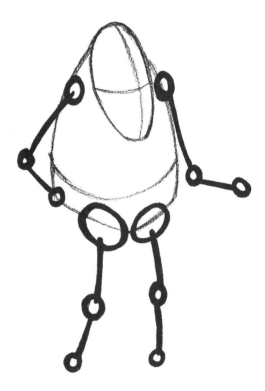

2 With guidelines, create his arms and legs. Use circles for the joints.

3 Begin to add head and facial features following the lines from step 1. Next, fill out his arms and legs by drawing around the guidelines. Use basic shapes to form the hands and feet. Make one of his hands a large hook as shown here. Erase the unneeded line in the lower part of his face as well as his hip joint circles.

4 Erase remaining unneeded lines, then begin to fill in the details. Draw in his unruly hair, beard, and sideburns. Sketch eyebrows, wrinkles, and teeth. Add his lab coat and belt, erasing lines as needed. Refine the shapes of his hand and his hook. Give him a pair of glasses.

5 You can finish Dr. Octagon Hex by drawing thin horizontal lines all over his body. Add any more details you wish— warts, wrinkles, and thin lips are a few ideas! Don't forget to put pockets on his lab coat. Use hatching and light and dark shading to define his head and coat.

These ghastly beings lurk in the swamps of many planets. Their slimy bodies act as perfect camouflage in their muddy, marshy environment. Those who are bitten by Mutant Swampzoids and survive turn into drippy green Swampzoids themselves!

1 Swampzoids have odd heads. Use a circle to get the shape of the top of the head and a pear shape for the face and jaws. A curved line will form the spine.

2 Connect the circle and pear shape to form the full shape of the Swampzoid's head. Make the chest with a rounded square shape drawn midway along its spine. Form its hips with a smaller shape at the base of the spine.

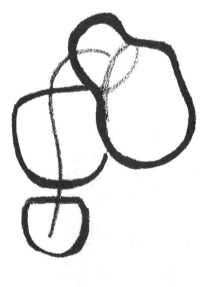

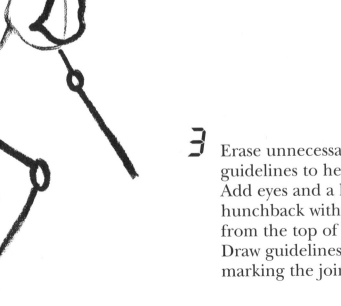

3 Erase unnecessary lines in head and draw guidelines to help place facial features. Add eyes and a large mouth. Give it a hunchback with a curved line that goes from the top of the head to the shoulder. Draw guidelines for its arms and legs, marking the joints with small circles.

4 Give it long, sharp, nasty-looking teeth. Fill out the limbs and body with wavy, wiggling lines to make it look blobby and drippy. Extend its mouth with a triangle at the side, and detail its left eye socket. Erase unneeded lines.

5 Now add even more wet, drippy, slushy layers with long teardrop shapes all over the Swampzoid. This will make it look extra wet and slimy! Be sure to sketch several drips flying off this mutant creature. Shade its gum line and darken inside its mouth and around its eyes.

REBLOZORTIX

Look out! The intelligent Reblozortix alien species considers human beings to be its natural enemy. These nasty creatures will become angry and hostile in your presence.

1 You'll need two shapes to draw this alien's head. Use an oval for the upper half and a shape below the oval for its mouth. Draw a line across the lower portion of the oval. Create a vertical line for its spine.

2 Add two eyes, and draw the upper body and hips. Sketch guidelines for the arms and legs, with circles at the joints. Outline its large three-fingered hands and three-toed feet.

3 Form its second pair of eyes by drawing circles above the head, connected by stalks to the forehead. Put in the brow line, and begin to draw lines to form the shape of its mouth. Outline its arms and legs, then connect the legs to the torso.

4 Outline the Reblozortix's eyestalks. Erase unneeded lines, then begin to add details. Use wrinkles around the snout, and add spots, bumps, and bony ridges on the body as needed. Flesh out the hands and feet with more defined lines, adding knuckles and wrinkles.

5 Last, add finishing touches to the Reblozortix. Darken inside its mouth, and add a drop of drool. Further define its upper eyes, leaving white highlights in the pupils. Detail this creature's lower torso with small curved lines. Use a minimal amount of shading on this lean, mean creature.

You are about to draw the King of the Galaxy. Lord Squid Von Squood is well liked on all planets, as he is considered a great leader and protector of his citizens. His only real enemies are Dr. Octagon Hex and those nasty old Reblozortix aliens.

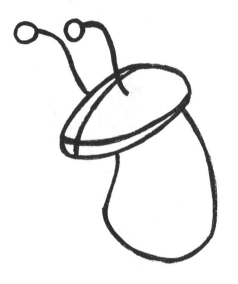

1 Start with an oval shape for his head. Use guidelines to find the center of his head. Draw a pearlike shape for his body. Make two circles for his eyeballs, attached to a pair of curved lines for the eyestalks.

2 Sketch guidelines for his arms, and add small circles at the joints. Make simple three-fingered hands. (You won't see the thumb on his left hand because of his position.) Flatten the lower edge of his body.

3 To add his tentacles, sketch in long squiggly lines that curl up at the ends. You can pose them any way you want.

4 Outline his arms. Draw his mouth, and put wrinkles around his lips and jawline. Outline the shape of his eyestalks, and attach eyelids around the circles of his eyes. Erase unneeded lines in his head.

5 Begin to erase guidelines in his eyestalks, face, torso, and arms. Add irises and pupils to his eyes. Draw four long, curved spines sticking out from the top of his head. Outline his tentacles.

6 Finish the spines on his head. Fill his mouth with tiny teeth. Draw some catfish-like tendrils dangling from his lower lip and forearms. Place wrinkles on his hands, and give him thin, bony fingers and knuckles. Erase the circles in his wrist joints. Don't forget to draw some wrinkles under his left arm.

7 To finish him up, continue to detail. You don't have to make your Lord Squid Von Squood look just like this one, but you may want to give your creature blotchy patterns, spots, or stripes like a fish or a reptile. Don't forget to finish his eyes with broken blood vessels. Add more wrinkles and bumps as you desire, especially to the fleshy area under his jaw.

Zigers make excellent pets. Highly intelligent, friendly, and large enough to ride on, they're also very protective of their masters. You'll always be safe with one of these powerful animals guarding your home, for few alien creatures are brave enough to fight a Ziger.

1 Start with the basic shape of the Ziger's head and a curving line to suggest its neck, back, and tail.

2 Add some guidelines as shown to determine the front, center, and side of its head. Draw a rounded shape for the body.

3 Sketch the visible eye, nostrils, and mouth. Draw two lines pointing straight up from its head for ears. Connect the head to the body with lines that go from the back of its head to the shoulders, then erase the original neckline. Start the Ziger's legs by drawing two ovals. Next, outline the tail.

4 Erase the guideline in the tail. Create eyelids, and put a pupil inside the eye. Outline its ears. The Ziger wears a bridle over its snout, like a horse, so draw two lines going around its snout just behind its nostrils. Give it long, pointed tusks curving out of its mouth. Use guidelines, circles, and triangular shapes for the legs and feet.

5 Add the curve of its cheek, and detail the insides of the ears. Outline the legs and feet, adding two toes on each foot. Erase the basic structure lines inside the legs, head, and body. Outline the saddle on the Ziger's back, and draw the basic shapes of a human figure sitting there.

6 Continue to sketch the rider. Connect his head to his shoulders, and use guidelines and circles to give him arms and a leg. Put a weapon in his hand. Further render the Ziger's face and feet.

7 Outline the Ziger's body with jagged lines to make it look furry. Put claws on its feet, and add the straps of the saddle that go under the Ziger's belly. Finish the rider's body and face. Draw the reins of the Ziger's bridle. Lastly, add a tuft of fur on the end of the Ziger's tail.

8 Erase the guidelines in the rider, and detail his costume as you wish. Now finish the Ziger. Darken its fur in places, as well as the claws, eye, and nostrils. Zigers look good with stripes—you can follow the example shown. Or, give your Ziger leopard spots or a black-and-white panda design—any pattern you can think of will work!

A young galactic gunslinger from Earth, Dirk Rocketboxer roams the spaceways looking for fortune and adventure. His battles with many evil aliens have made Dirk both an outlaw and a hero on several planets.

1 Draw an oval for Dirk's head. Fill it out with structure lines, then sketch in his nose and mouth. For his spine, make a curved vertical line that extends down from his head. Draw a simple shape for Dirk's upper body and another for his pelvis.

2 Using the structure lines, draw Dirk's eyes and eyebrows. Sketch his ear. Start drawing his arms, legs, hands, and feet using guidelines and simple shapes. Draw small circles for the joints.

3 Erase the horizontal guideline in his face. Draw his spiky hair. Next, outline his arms and legs. Form his hands, complete with knuckles and individual fingers. Create his neck by drawing a half-circle under his jawline. Draw his suit cuffs.

4 Erase unneeded guidelines. Be sure to leave a jagged line down the right side of his face for his scar. Begin to draw his uniform, and develop the shapes of his combat boots. Start to sketch his guns, using rectangles for the barrels.

5 Put a backpack on his back. This pack stores the energy for his guns, so draw power cables going from the guns to the backpack. Detail his clothing, boots, and both guns.

6 Use short hatching lines to finish the power cables. Shade Dirk as you wish to add texture and shadows. Darken his hair and boots. Dirk looks ready for action, doesn't he?

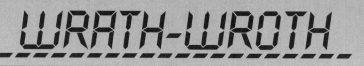

These big furry monsters are cute when they're pups, but they grow up to be vicious predators that will eat any living thing in sight!

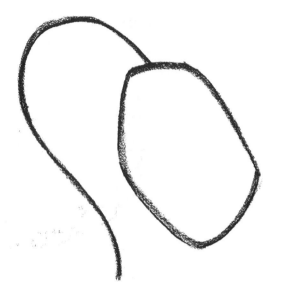

1 Start with the basic shape of its head and the spine curve.

2 Draw the round shapes of its upper body and pelvis. Add circles for its right shoulder and its hips. Draw its facial features, including the extra-large mouth.

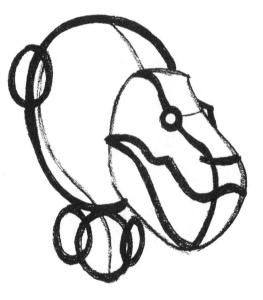

3 Use guidelines to draw its arms and legs. Place circles at the joints. Use simple shapes and lines to create its hands and feet. Draw the nostrils and the curve of its cheek, which slightly overlaps its body. Erase any unneeded lines in the face. Shape its left shoulder.

4 Outline all the limbs, connecting everything to form the Wrath-Wroth's body. Add claws to its hands and feet. Put big sharp teeth inside its mouth. Further shape its eyes and nostrils. Indicate its jaw muscles by drawing a line that goes from the top jaw to the bottom jaw. Erase the face and spine guidelines.

5 Erase unneeded lines in the legs, arms, and pelvis. Draw a jagged edge around the outline of the Wrath-Wroth's body to make it look furry. Put tiny circles in its muzzle under the nostrils.

6 To add the final touches, shade the Wrath-Wroth. Sketch long lines all over it to suggest a long, shaggy fur coat. Finish its beady eyes. Give it whiskers, and darken inside its nostrils and mouth. Since it's a savage meat-eater, you may want to have it drooling and foaming at the mouth.

43

For speedy interplanetary travel, there is no faster mode of transportation than the Space Train. Fast, safe, and sleek, the Space Train is also more efficient than the old locomotive, which tended to whip-snap its tail end into asteroids and lose passenger cars.

1 Draw a square shape for the front of the train. Then add a long curved line trailing back.

2 Draw two more lines, one coming from the top-right corner and another from the bottom-left corner of the square. These two lines should meet at the tail end of the first line.

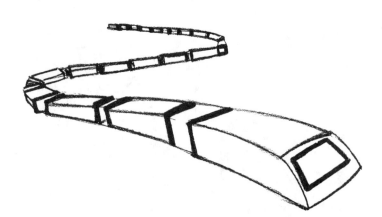

3 Draw a small square inside the first square for the front windshield. To separate the different cars on the train, make a series of angled lines that go straight across the top of the train, hit the corner edge, and go to the train base. Make them in sets of two, then erase the structure lines in between. Use simple lines to separate the cars at the back of the train.

4 Begin to detail with windows in the front train cars. Between each car, draw smaller cube shapes for the junctions, which connect the train cars. Draw zigzag lines slanted across the windshield to suggest light reflecting off the glass. Sketch a rectangular shape along the side of the first car for a window. Add a triangular shape behind it for an engine. Finally, draw a line going down the center of the first car's roof.

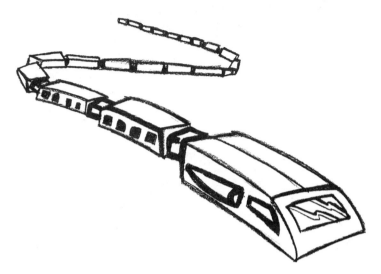

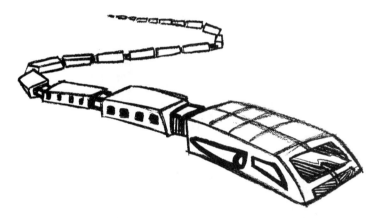

5 Draw lines going across the roof of the first car to suggest heavy-duty metal plating. Darken the windshield, except for the reflection. Add a grille on the front, below the windshield, using a simple rectangle with slanted lines inside. Sketch vertical lines on the side of the first junction.

6 Finally, shade the train by making the sides dark and leaving the top light in places. You can put small lines, dots, and other marks all over the train to indicate dents and scratches from years of travel. For the background, add asteroids, planets, or even Zip Cars to fill your scene.

Well-armed Fighter Blasters are perfect two-man ships for police patrol or, if necessary, all-out ship-to-ship combat. Fighter Blasters are seen all over the galaxy, keeping Lord Squid Von Squood's kingdom as crime free as possible.

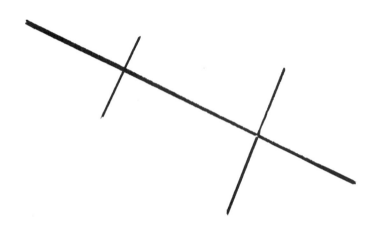

1 With a ruler, draw one long line at a slant to mark the center of the ship. Add two shorter lines to show the ship's width.

2 Using the lines you drew in step 1, create the basic outline of the ship. You may want to use a ruler to get some of the lines straight.

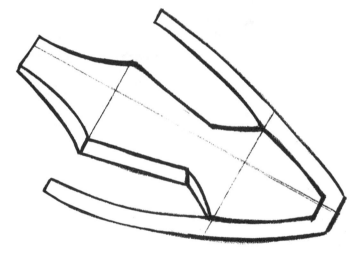

3 Next, draw the wings and the front windshield as shown.

4 Begin to detail the front piece, the midsection, and the tail of the ship. Add windows to the top and sides of the windshield. Erase unneeded guidelines.

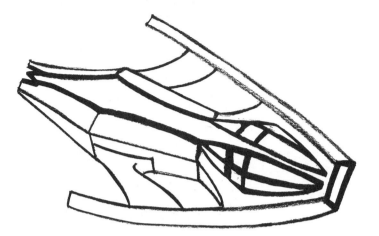

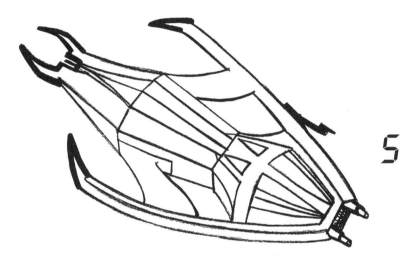

5 Sketch points to complete the ends of the wings and tail rudders. Draw a cannon on one side of the ship and two small cannons at the front.

6 Erase any unneeded lines. Shade the ship, then add some fine details, including a few dents and pockmarks from past adventures. By shading certain sections only, you will create a three-dimensional effect.

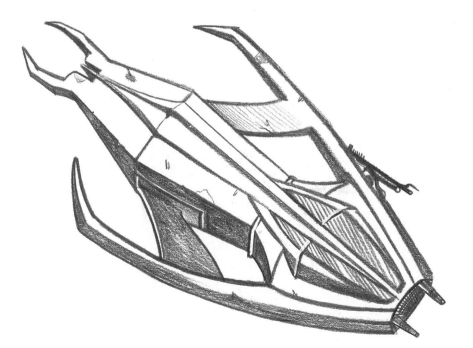

On the planet Mercury, there exists a society of mutated insects that ride around on giant spiders, fiercely protecting their territory and hunting for prey. Be on the lookout!

1 Start with a small oval for the head and a larger pointed oval for the abdomen of the giant spider. Using large and small circles, draw the spider's 10 eyes on its head. On the body, draw four small circles where its left legs attach. Sketch four short lines to create the parts of its mouth.

2 Fill out the shapes of its mouth parts. Draw eight long, spiny, bent legs.

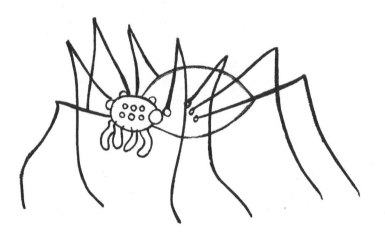

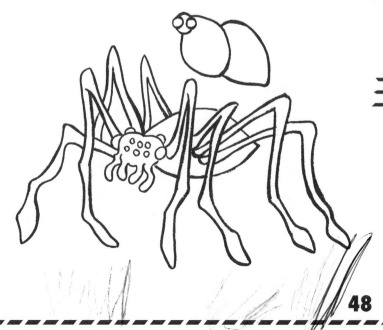

3 Fill out the shapes of the legs, using the lines in step 2 as a guide. Sketch the Spider Rider's eyes, head, and body. Erase unneeded lines in the spider.

4 Put arms and legs on the Spider Rider. Place a spear in its right hand, and make its left hand hold the reins attached to the spider. Suggest the rider's mouth, then erase its unneeded lines.

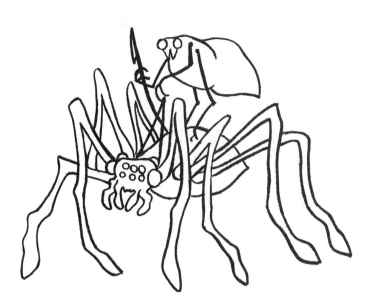

5 Now to add detail! Outline the rider's arms and legs. Create the texture of fur with zigzag lines around the legs and bodies of the rider and the spider. With hatching, shade the undersides of both creatures. Continue to detail as you wish.

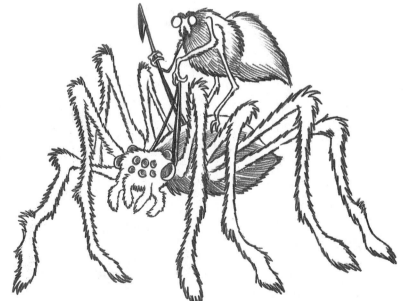

The ugliest monster in the universe is also one of the most deadly. Thank goodness it is only found in one place: on the seventh ring of Saturn.

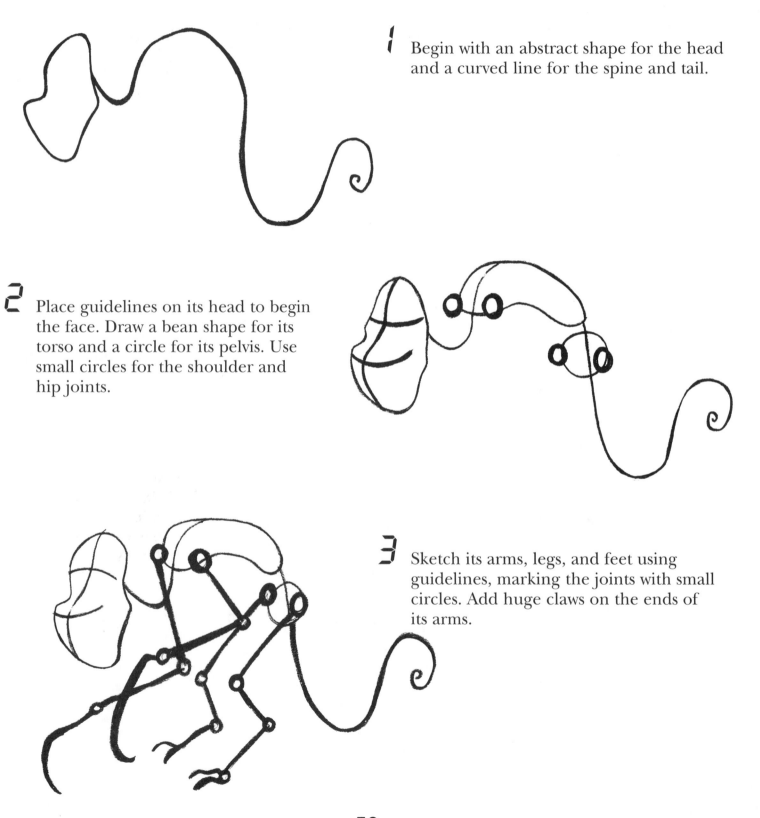

1 Begin with an abstract shape for the head and a curved line for the spine and tail.

2 Place guidelines on its head to begin the face. Draw a bean shape for its torso and a circle for its pelvis. Use small circles for the shoulder and hip joints.

3 Sketch its arms, legs, and feet using guidelines, marking the joints with small circles. Add huge claws on the ends of its arms.

4 Draw the hideous facial features as shown. Erase unneeded lines in face. Add a jagged line around the top of its head, back, and tail. This is the monster's bristly, furry mane.

5 Draw frightening teeth. Using the guidelines, outline its neck, arms, legs, claws, and feet. The hand claws should have a jagged edge. Also sketch the underside of its tail. Erase unneeded lines.

6 Draw lines around its neck, belly, and tail to create the look of segmented, buglike armor plating. Further define the Skraggle-Zaggle's arms, legs, and head.

7 To make this Skraggle-Zaggle your own creation, play with different finishing techniques. Smooth-tone shading combined with hatching for darker areas makes for a supercool, superugly monster. Or try one of the other techniques described on pages 6 and 7.

Very difficult to fly, these small, one-pilot fighter ships are designed and flown by the Reblozortix aliens. Many bold Reblozortix attacks have been thwarted by malfunctioning Invader Ships, which have—on more than one occasion—exploded for no apparent reason.

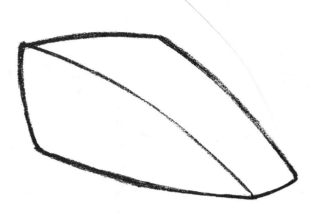

1 Draw a wedge shape. Add a slightly curved line to give it a three-dimensional quality.

2 Using triangular shapes, add a tail fin, windshield, and side engine.

3 Add two more triangular side fins. Create two rectangular shapes to begin the wings.

4 Extend the side wings. To make the top fin and side wings appear three-dimensional, draw thin pairs of lines as shown. Erase unneeded lines. Add three small guns to the front of the ship, and detail the side engine.

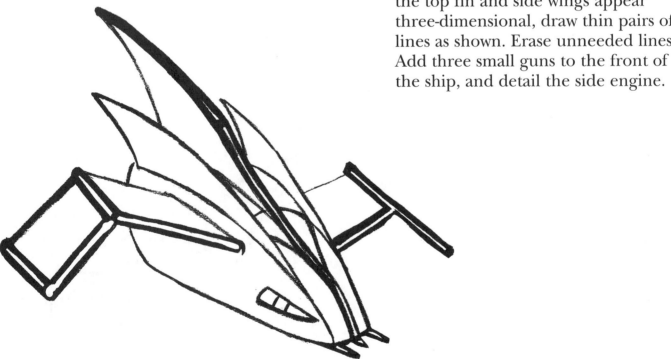

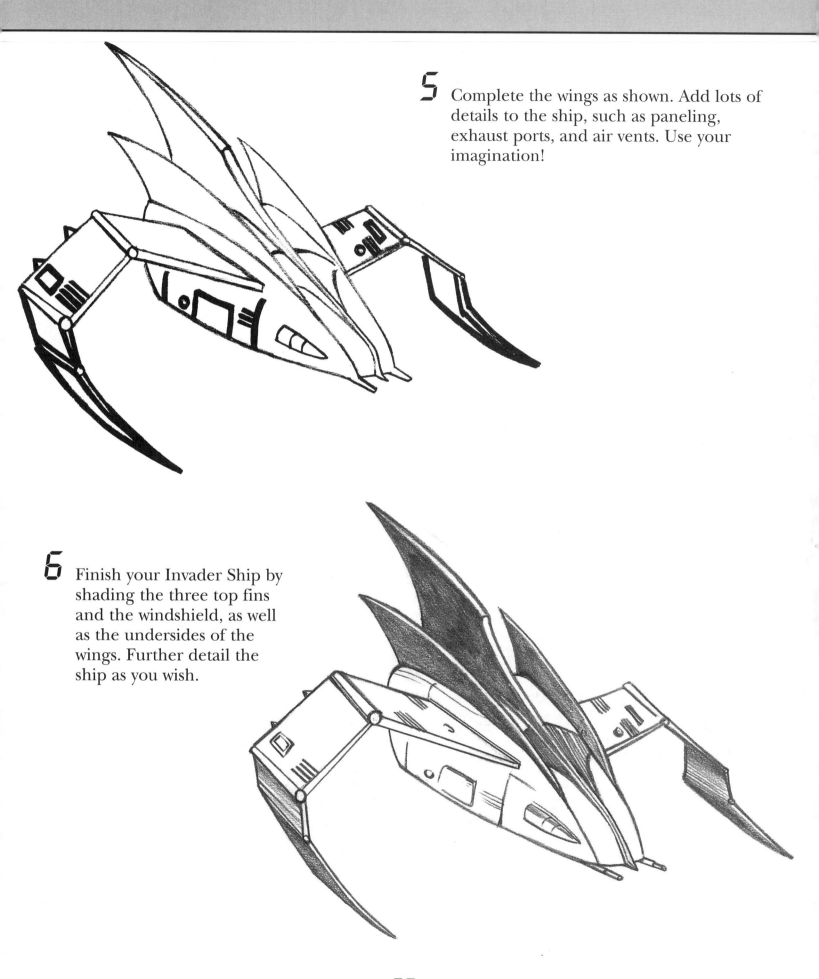

5 Complete the wings as shown. Add lots of details to the ship, such as paneling, exhaust ports, and air vents. Use your imagination!

6 Finish your Invader Ship by shading the three top fins and the windshield, as well as the undersides of the wings. Further detail the ship as you wish.

These intelligent reptilian beings inhabit the tropical regions of several planets. They are helpful to alienkind because they eat many types of harmful creatures—including Mutant Swampzoids, Martian Lobster Monsters, and Reblozortix aliens!

1 Start with a basic bullet shape for the head and guidelines for the spine, shoulders, and hips.

2 Create rounded shapes for the torso and hips, as well as small circles for the shoulder and hip joints.

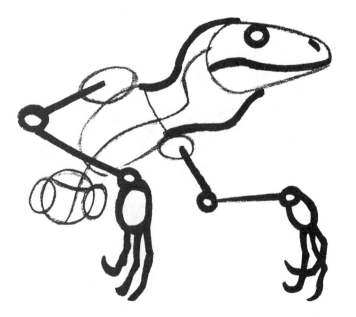

3 Sketch the eye, nostril, and mouth. With guidelines, connect the head to the shoulders. Form the arms, hands, and fingers with guidelines and circles.

4 Use lines to create the spines on its head and neck. Continue to detail the face and jawline. Use small triangles for the teeth. With guidelines, draw the legs, feet, and tail. Use circles for the joints. Flesh out the arms and clawed hands.

5 Complete the shape of its neck, legs, feet, and tail. Further detail its head. Begin to add clothing. Erase unneeded lines in the body and arms.

6 Erase extra lines in its legs and tail. Continue to detail the lizard's clothing and feet.

7 Begin to add scales with small *V* shapes around the head and cross-hatching under the neck and tail. Don't forget the alien lizard's eyelashes.

8 Last, shade the character, then add your own details. More scales, more spikes, more stripes—it's up to you!

What happens to astronauts who get sucked into black holes? They turn into horrible zombies—Cosmic Creeps—who come back to haunt the spaceways and eat anyone they encounter.

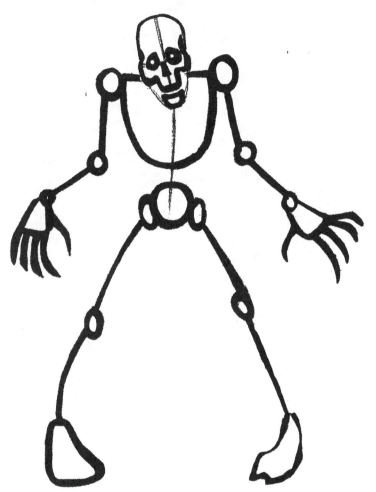

1 Make an oval for the head, and draw guidelines. Add one long line for the Cosmic Creep's spine. Place his nose hole in the center of his head, where the guidelines cross. Put eye sockets on either side of the nose hole. Add the curved lines of his cheekbones, temples, and mouth. Draw basic shapes for his chest and hips. Use guidelines for his arms and legs, with small circles at the joints. Simple shapes can be used to form his hands and feet. Add thin lines for his fingers.

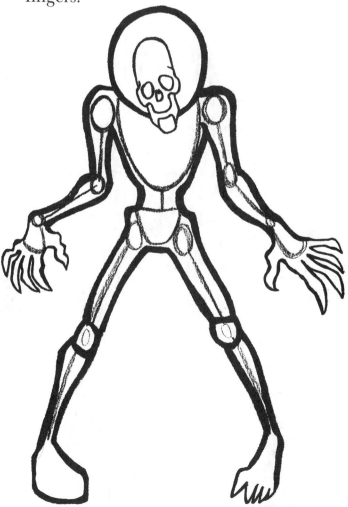

2 Erase the guidelines in the face and torso. Draw a large circle around the Cosmic Creep's skull to form his round space helmet. Outline his arms, hands, body, legs, and feet. Make one foot round like a boot, and draw pointed skeleton toes on the other foot. Place circles on his knees for the knee pads of his suit.

3 Go around the skull with jagged lines to make the hole where his space helmet has been shattered. Draw curved lines coming out of his helmet for air tubes. Sketch parallel lines that cross his body for the straps of his space suit. Use more zigzag lines around his arms and legs for his torn, tattered clothing. Begin to fill in the details of his boot.

4 Erase unneeded lines. Add scraggly hair around his skull and more torn clothing around his body. Outline his air tubes, and add more details to his foot, boot, and space suit. Don't forget to detail his hideous mouth.

5 Now that you have the basic form of the Cosmic Creep, begin to detail him. Place wrinkles in his clothing and lines on the air tubes and the straps of his suit. Further define his hands and foot. Add eyeballs to his eye sockets, and darken his mouth. Don't forget the watch on his left hand.

6 Finish your Cosmic Creep with more scary details: a slobbering chin, bulging eyeballs, torn tendons—add whatever you dare! Use hatching and shading to "bring him to life"!

Here are more tips on how to put life into your drawings. Keep in mind that the most realistic drawings combine several finishing techniques. You can practice and experiment with your own favorite combinations!

CONTOUR DRAWING

Even if you don't plan to fill in your drawing with color or texture, you can make your object or character look more solid by changing the darkness and width of its outlines. For example, note the difference in the line weight within the drawing of Dr. Octagon Hex. The lower edges of his lab coat are thicker to suggest shadows. Also, whenever a line bends or meets another line, it thickens. This technique not only makes the character appear more three-dimensional, but it also makes the drawing more fun to look at.

CAST SHADOWS

The simplest thing you can do to make your drawing look rounded and real is to give it a shadow. To do this, you must imagine where the shadow of its form would be if the creature were resting on a flat surface with light coming from above. Notice that the shaded areas on Lord Squid Von Squood show that the light source comes from above and in front of him. His arms and tentacles are casting shadows directly underneath themselves.

LIGHT FIGURE, DARK BACKGROUND

You'll be surprised by how rounded your creature will look if you simply darken the space behind it. By darkening the space behind this Mutant Swampzoid, you can create a rounded, three-dimensional effect.

Don't forget, once you've figured out how to draw these monsters, you can go back and draw them again, changing the details to make a unique version all your own. Follow the same steps we've shown you to add a different number of eyes, arms, legs, or whatever you can imagine.

And once you've learned how to draw a couple of different monsters, you can rearrange all of their body parts—putting the head of one kind of monster onto another's body, or making two-headed aliens, or whatever you choose. If you can follow our steps, you can always combine them in different ways to make up some totally weird things.

BACKGROUNDS

Once you have completed a drawing, you may want to put your creature or vehicle in a setting. For many of your illustrations, the background can be outer space, but you can add all sorts of things to make the scenery interesting. Use your imagination! Here are some suggestions for creating different settings.

MAGAZINE BACKGROUNDS

If you like to cut and paste, ask your family for some old magazines you can cut up. Cut out pictures of different patterns and trim them so they're shaped like craters, rocks, a cave, or even an alien cityscape. This will give your picture an interesting abstract look. And you don't have to fill the entire page. A few groupings to the side or below your main drawing will give the impression of a whole scene.

PAINTED BACKGROUNDS

You don't need a paintbrush to add painted backgrounds! To create small craters on a planet's surface, dip the end of a drinking straw into some paint and print tiny indentation pockets around your alien. You can make smaller craters by using the ends of tiny pieces of macaroni, or bigger ones with large pieces. Cut a piece of sponge, dip it in paint, and stamp it onto your picture to create a rock texture. A crumpled piece of waxed paper or a paper towel can achieve the same effect. Be sure not to get these too wet, though, or they won't work well. Look around the house for other printing tools, such as old wooden spools, corrugated cardboard, or cut pieces of Styrofoam.

TEXTURED BACKGROUNDS

If you want to create a textured background, you'll need to draw your space alien or vehicle on a thin piece of paper. Place a textured object (such as sandpaper) under the section of your paper where you want the texture to appear. Now grab a pencil with a soft lead. Using the side of the pencil lead, rub lightly and evenly over the area. For other cool textures, try using window screening, rough wood, a kitchen grater—anything you can imagine!

SHADOWED BACKGROUNDS

By adding shadows in the right places, your illustrations will leap off the page! Imagine where the shadow of your alien or vehicle would fall underneath itself. Then fill in those areas with a dark pencil. You might want to add shadows to some of the rocks or background scenery, too. When adding shadows to your backgrounds, remember that sunlight is different at different times of the day. Morning and late-afternoon light make objects cast very long shadows. Whenever the sun is directly overhead, the shadows cast are very short.